CHILDREN IN HISTORY
The Victorians

Kate Jackson-Bedford

W
FRANKLIN WATTS
LONDON·SYDNEY

First published in 2009 by
Franklin Watts
338 Euston Road
London NW1 3BH

Franklin Watts Australia
Hachette Children's Books
Level 17/207 Kent Street
Sydney NSW 2000

ISBN 978 0 7496 8699 4
Dewey classification: 941.081

Series Editor: Jeremy Smith
Art director: Jonathan Hair
Design: Jane Hawkins
Cover Design: Jane Hawkins
Picture research: Diana Morris

Picture credits: Art Archive: front cover tr.
Mary Evans Picture Library: 4c, 5b, 6b, 12c, 17,
19t, 24c, 24b, 25t, 26bl, 26cr, 30ct, 30b.
Mary Evans Picture Library/Alamy: 7.
Fine Art PL/Corbis: 1, 11t. Fotomas/Topham:
8t, 8b, 12t, 13, 22tl, 23, 24tl, 25b, 30t, 30c. R
Gates/Hulton Archive/Getty Images: 22cr.
Margo Harrison/Shutterstock: 5t.
Hulton-Deutsch/Corbis: 18t, 18cr.
Svetlana Larina/Shutterstock: 11cb.
The London Art Archive/Alamy: 6t
Nigel Paul Monkton/Shutterstock: 11b.
Museum of London/HIP/Topfoto: 10t, 10b.
National Archives: 19b. National
Archives/HIP/Topfoto: 15, 22bl. Paper
Rodeo/Corbis: 18bl. Picturepoint/Topham: front
cover tc, 2, 3, 4tl, 4b, 14tl, 14bl, 16t, 16b, 20tl,
20b,21. Popperfoto/Getty Images: 26tl, 27.
Mark William Richardson/Shutterstock: 9
Ann Ronan Picture Library / HIP/Topfoto:
front cover b. Amoret Tanner/Alamy: 14cr.
Topfoto: front cover tl. V/Shutterstock: 11c.
City of Westminster Archive Centre,
London/Bridgeman Art Library: 20c.
T. R. Williams/William Grundy/London
Stereoscopic Company/Getty Images: 8c.

A CIP catalogue record for this book is
available from the British Library

Franklin Watts is a division of
Hachette Children's Books, an
Hachette UK company.
www.hachette.co.uk

Printed in China

Note to parents and teachers: Every effort has
been made by the Publishers to ensure that the
websites detailed at the back of this book are
suitable for children, that they are of the
highest educational value, and that they
contain no inappropriate or offensive material.
However, because of the nature of the Internet,
it is impossible to guarantee that the contents
of these sites will not be altered. We strongly
advise that Internet access is supervised by a
responsible adult.

Contents

The Victorian age

The Victorian era began in 1837, when Victoria became queen and lasted until her death in 1901. Children who lived during this time are called Victorian children. During Queen Victoria's long reign, children's lives changed in many ways.

Changing Britain

When Victoria first became queen, most people lived and worked in the countryside. This changed when thousands of families moved to the growing towns to find jobs and work in the new factories. By the end of the Victorian times, 70 per cent of the population lived in the towns.

▲ The smoke from factory chimneys made towns dirty and polluted.

▲ People worked long hours in factories.

An industrial nation

Britain became an industrial nation using the new steam engines to power machines in factories that made cotton and other goods. Trading these goods with countries all over the world changed Britain into a rich and powerful nation.

4

Steam power

Steam power was also used to power trains on the new railways that were built all over the country. By 1900, 35,000 km of track had been built all over Britain.

▶ The new railways made it possible for people to travel further and faster than ever before.

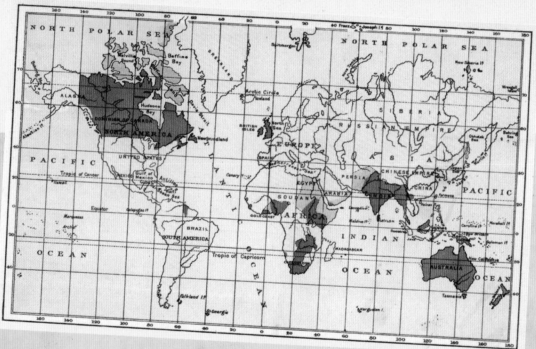

◀ The 'pink' areas of the world were ruled by Britain in 1901.

Great Empire

Britain took control of many other countries during Victorian times. The Victorians believed they could improve these countries and they also wanted to trade with them to make Britain wealthy. By 1901 the area controlled by Britain covered more than one quarter of the Earth's surface. It was known as the British Empire.

Victorian families

Victorian children led different lives depending on which sort of family they came from. Children born into rich families had comfortable, sheltered lives while children of poor families lived a hard life.

Which class?

Victorian society was divided into three social classes according to how wealthy people were. The upper class, who were very rich, powerful and didn't have to work, included the royal family, lords and ladies. A wide range of people such as doctors, bankers, school teachers, shop keepers and office workers, were in the middle class. The lower or working class worked as servants or did hard manual labour in places such as mines, factories or farms.

▲ In poor families, children had to share the same bed with their brothers and sisters.

Short lives

In Victorian times it was common for poor children to die before they were five years old, often from fatal diseases they caught by drinking polluted water. The crowded homes where they lived helped to spread diseases from family to family.

▲ Working class children admire a beautifully dressed upper class girl.

Bigger families

Victorian parents had much larger families than we do today. Often mothers had a new baby each year. We can see how many children Victorian families had by looking at the census information (now held on computer). It shows the names and ages of the children living at home.

▶ This computer print-out of a Victorian census shows that the Darby family had seven children.

NAME	RELATION	MARITAL STATUS	GENDER	AGE	BIRTHPLACE	OCCUPATION
HENRY DARBY	HEAD	M	MALE	41	ISLE OF WIGHT, HAMPSHIRE, ENGLAND	TINPLATE WORKER
GRACE DARBY	WIFE	M	FEMALE	42	NORTHAMPTON, ENGLAND	
JOHN DARBY	SON		MALE	19	LONDON, LONDON, MIDDLESEX, ENGLAND	TINPLATE WORKER
WALTER DARBY	SON		MALE	17	LONDON, LONDON, MIDDLESEX, ENGLAND	TINPLATE WORKER
THOMAS DARBY	SON		MALE	14	ISLINGTON	TINPLATE WORKER
GEORGE DARBY	SON		MALE	10	ISLINGTON	SCHOLAR
JESSIE DARBY	DAUGHTER		FEMALE	8	ISLINGTON	SCHOLAR
ELLEN DARBY	DAUGHTER		FEMALE	4	ISLINGTON	SCHOLAR
FREDERICK DARBY	SON		MALE	1	ISLINGTON	

Who looked after the children?

Rich and middle class children were looked after by a hired nanny who lived with the family. The children would spend most of their time with her in the nursery and often saw their parents only once a day for a short while. Poor children were often looked after by a grandmother, an older brother or sister because their parents were out working all day.

◀ Wealthy children often knew their nanny (such as the one shown here) better than their parents.

A place to live

Home for a Victorian child could be a grand mansion or just one room in a house. Where they lived depended on which class they belonged to. Some children didn't have a home at all and lived on the streets.

Grand mansion

Upper class families often had two homes. A grand house in London and a mansion surrounded by gardens and large grounds in the countryside. Their houses had many rooms and needed lots of servants to do all the work. The children's rooms were on the top floor where they had their own nursery, schoolroom, bedrooms and bathroom.

◀ These lucky Victorian children lived in this grand, comfortable mansion.

Cramped and crowded

The homes of working class, town children were small brick houses built in long rows called terraces. These houses had no piped water and families had to share an outside toilet with others on the street. Very poor families lived in just one rented room in dirty, damp, overcrowded houses known as the slums.

▶ These children are playing outside terraced houses in East London.

Middle class home

The children of bankers or doctors lived in villas. These homes had enough rooms for the family and servants. There was running water, an inside bathrooom and gas lighting. The homes were decorated with rugs, velvet curtains and flowery wallpaper.

▶ Middle class houses often had three to four storeys and could be detached or terraced houses (shown right).

VICTORIAN LEGACY

Homes today

Many people still live in Victorian houses today. Now these homes have been improved and have running water, indoor bathrooms and electricity. Look out for rows of Victorian terraced brick houses which have two rooms upstairs and two downstairs. Middle class houses are bigger, often have bay windows at the front, patterned brickwork and stained glass in the doors.

Meal times

It is important to eat a good diet to keep healthy. Many Victorian children didn't eat enough food to get the nutrients to grow strong. They were usually small and thin and undernourished.

Poor diet

Many working class families couldn't afford to buy enough food and their children often went hungry. The meals they ate were mainly bread, potatoes and sometimes a little bacon and vegetables. A child's breakfast was often milk with a slice of bread spread thinly with butter or dripping. If they were lucky they might have porridge with a spoonful of treacle.

A poor diet

An interview with an eight-year-old girl who sold watercress on the streets of London in 1851 shows what a poor diet she had. The food she ate was not enough to give her the nutrients and energy she needed. She must have been very hungry.

"I don't have no dinner. Mother gives me two slices of bread and butter and a cup of tea for breakfast and then I go till tea and has the same."

Published in *London Labour and the London Poor* by Henry Mayhew (1857)

◀ These children are queuing for a 'farthing breakfast', which consisted of a mug of cocoa and a bun.

Good food

Children in rich and middle class families had plenty of food. Breakfast was often eggs or bread and milk. Dinner, at noon, was meat and potatoes with a pudding or stewed fruit. Tea was bread, jam and cake. Finally biscuits and milk were served for supper.

◀ A servant brings a meal to a child in her nursery.

In the country

Families who lived in the country were able to produce some of their own food. They grew vegetables in their garden. Some families kept a cow to provide milk, chickens to give eggs, bees for honey and even kept a pig to fatten and kill for eating. Children helped to gather free wild foods such as blackberries, nuts and mushrooms.

▶ These foods all grow wild, so everyone could harvest them.

mushrooms

blackberries

hazel nuts

Going to school

When Victoria became queen, most children did not go to school. Parents could pay for charity schools, but for many families this was too expensive. By the end of the Victorian era, schools were free and compulsory.

Learning at home

Wealthy children were taught at home by a governess or private tutor. When boys were ten years old they were sent to boarding schools, such as Eton or Rugby, where they were educated to become leaders. There were very few schools for girls, so most were kept at home and taught reading, writing, sewing, drawing and music.

▲ Wealthy children were taught at home until the age of ten or older.

Writing things down

Children first learned to write by tracing letters in sand trays with a finger. Later they wrote on slates using a special pencil. When they had finished, the slate was wiped clean with a wet cloth and used again. Older children wrote on paper using wooden pens with steel nibs which had to be dipped in ink every few words.

slate

inkwell

pen

◀ Victorian writing equipment used by children in school.

Lesson Time

Victorian schools often taught boys and girls in separate classes. They were mainly taught the 3Rs, Reading, wRiting and aRithmetic, with some geography, history and drill. The teaching was dull because most of the learning was done by reciting things, like facts and times tables, over and over again until children knew them by heart.

▼ Children sat in long rows of desks facing the blackboard and teacher.

Schools

Children go to school today because of the laws made by the Victorians. They also left us the legacy of many Victorian school buildings which are still used today. For example, there are clues that show if a school is Victorian. The date it was built is carved in brickwork and there are separate labelled doors for boys and girls.

Working for a living

The wages paid to poor people were low, so families needed their children to work as soon as they could. Many children helped their mothers, who worked from home, making matchboxes or brooms.

In the factory

Many children worked in factories making things like cloth. The owners liked employing children because they could be paid less than adults and they were small enough to crawl under moving machines to clean or mend broken threads. Factory work was dangerous and accidents were common.

▲ Chimney sweeps were small and thin to fit inside the narrow chimneys. This sweep's cheerful expression disguises the fact this was tough, dirty work.

Chimney sweeps

Victorian houses were heated with coal or wood fires which filled their tall chimneys with soot. Boys and girls were sent up inside the dirty, twisting chimneys to clean out the soot which couldn't be reached with brushes. They climbed up by pressing their knees and elbows against the walls. Sometimes children got stuck or fell into fires.

▲ Some children worked long hours in factories, such as this young girl.

Going underground

In the 1840s, boys and girls as young as four years old were employed in mines. Among other things, they worked as trappers and had to sit alone in the dark opening ventilation doors for the coal wagons to go through. Trappers had to be careful not to fall asleep in case they fell on the track and were injured.

▶ Girl miners get ready to go down the pits in Wigan, England. There were hundreds of girls and women who worked the Lancashire coalfields in the 19th century. They were nicknamed 'pit brow lasses'.

VICTORIAN LEGACY

Laws to stop child labour

A reformer called Lord Shaftesbury helped to change and improve Victorian children's lives. He persuaded Parliament to make new laws that governed how children worked. The laws raised the age children started work, shortened the number of hours they worked and stopped children working down mines and as chimney sweeps. By the end of the Victorian era, most children did not work and went to school instead. Today, it is illegal for children below the age of 14 to work at all.

Country life

The children of men who worked on farms were used to moving home because farm workers homes usually went with their job. The cottages they lived in were small and damp with an outdoor privy.

Farm work

▲ A bird rattle used to scare birds away from crops.

Farm workers wages were low so children had to help earn extra money. Girls did jobs like stone picking and weeding. Young boys were employed as bird scarers who had to frighten birds away from crops by making a noise with a wooden rattle. Older boys worked with the large horses that pulled the ploughs and carts. This was dangerous work because the boys were not strong enough to control the huge horses.

Harvest time

Country children helped with the harvest. They earned money picking fruit or helping to harvest the corn or hay. Young children helped their mothers with gleaning. This was collecting the corn left behind in the field after the harvester had gone. The family then had the corn ground into flour at the local mill and used it at home to bake bread and cakes.

▶ Children are helping to harvest hay in Somerset.

Days off school

Country children often missed school because they were working on farms. School logbooks were kept by the headteacher and they recorded when children were away and why. This text from a logbook from Kelvedon Hatch school in Essex shows the type of work children were doing instead of going to school.

Jan - plough driving

Feb - planting seeds

Mar - bird scarring, dropping peas, potato planting

April - stone picking

June - bird scaring, fruit picking, hay making, pea picking

July - fruit picking, hay making, taking dinner to fathers in the fields, pea picking

Aug - corn harvest

Sept - gleaning, blackberrying, potato picking

Oct - blackberrying, acorn collecting, gleaning, gathering sloes, apple picking, potato picking

Life on a canal boat

Some children lived with their families on long canal boats. They travelled on their boat up and down the canals of Britain carrying things like coal from the coal mines to the factories. Canal boat children did not go to school because they never stayed in one place for long. They had to help work the locks on the canal and look after the horse that pulled the canal boat.

▼ Children helped by leading the horse along the tow path beside the canal.

In trouble

Victorian parents expected their children to be well behaved. Children had to do as they were told and be seen and not heard. Children who behaved badly were punished.

Victorian Sundays

Many Victorian families kept Sunday as a day of rest and went to church. For the rest of the day children were expected to play very quietly with religious toys, such as a Noah's ark, or study the Bible. In some families children were not allowed to play at all and could only pray and study the Bible.

Children's rhyme - :
> I must not play on Sunday
> Because it is a sin.
> Tomorrow it will be Monday
> and then I can begin.

This rhyme reminded Victorian children not to play on a Sunday.

▲ Children in 'Sunday Best' outside their local church.

▼ Children were often shamed in front of their classmates.

School rules

Discipline in Victorian schools was very strict. Pupils who misbehaved were punished by being hit with a cane or leather strap. Children who found learning difficult were shamed in front of the whole class. They had to stand on a stool wearing a cone shaped hat called a dunce's hat.

Against the law

Many poor or homeless children got into trouble with the law. At the start of the Victorian era, child criminals were treated the same as adults and could be whipped and sent to prison. If the crime was bad enough, children as young as ten years old could face the death penalty or be transported to Van Dieman's land, an island south of Australia, now called Tasmania.

▶ Children were put in prison with tough adult criminals.

Hard labour

Victorian prison records from Wandsworth Prison in London, show us the crimes children committed and how they were punished. Thirteen-year-old Henry Munday (right), stole 14 lb of sugar in May 1873. He was punished with a whipping and four days hard labour which could have been work such as breaking up stones.

19

Hard times

The very poorest Victorian families had no home. They had the choice of going into a workhouse or living on the streets. Workhouses were hated places. Life was made very hard for the people living in them.

The workhouse

When a family entered a workhouse they were split up. The mother and father were separated into men and women's areas. Often children were kept apart from their mother. Everyone wore uniforms and slept in dormitories. Adults had to do hard work such as crushing bones to make glue. Children had to attend the workhouse school and often helped with work too.

▲ Children had to sew and mend things in the workhouse.

Street children

Many children were orphans because their parents had died of disease or in accidents. They lived on the streets begging, stealing or doing odd jobs to earn a few pennies to buy food. During the 1850s, up to 30,000 children lived on the streets of London.

◄ Street children dressed in rags and survived on scraps.

Dr Barnardo

Dr Thomas Barnardo was shocked by the number of children he saw sleeping rough in London. He started homes for street children where they got food, shelter and training. Girls learned domestic skills and boys a craft or trade, so that when they left the home they would be able to find a job to support themselves.

▶ Thousands of children like these were rescued from life on the streets.

Victorian charities

Charities, such as Barnardo's and the NSPCC, were founded to help Victorian children, and they are still helping children today. The NSPCC started in 1884 with the aim of stopping the ill-treatment of children. Today, the charity still follows that aim and helps children through schemes such as Childline, which young people can telephone to talk about their problems.

Dressed up

Victorian children dressed like smaller versions of their parents. Their clothes were usually uncomfortable, heavy and not designed to play in. It was possible to tell which social class children belonged to by the clothes they wore.

Grand clothes

Wealthy children had new clothes made for them at a dressmakers or bought from a shop. Boys wore dresses until they were five years old and then changed to knee length trousers and jackets, often made of velvet with a lace collar. Girls wore smaller versions of their mother's grand dresses.

▲ Poor children 'padded out' their clothes with newspaper in the winter in order to stay warm.

Second hand

In middle class families, adult clothes were sometimes cut down to make children's clothes. Outfits were passed down from child to child. Poor children wore clothes that had been passed down many times and were patched and ragged. In the winter, they stuffed clothes with newspaper to stay warm.

▲ Sailor suits, like this boy is wearing, became fashionable after Queen Victoria's eldest son wore one.

From top to toe

In Victorian times it was considered respectable to wear a hat, so most children wore one. Shoes were an expensive luxury for poor families. Like clothes, boots were handed down and would be mended over and over again. Some children wore wooden clogs, but many went barefoot even in winter.

◄ Poor children often had to go barefoot in the winter, including this poor girl.

In Uniform

Records show that children went into Gressenhall workhouse in Norfolk, their own clothes were taken away from them. Instead they had to wear a uniform of the same type of dresses for all the girls and the same shirts, jackets and trousers for all the boys. Gressenhall workhouse had its own shoemaker, so children were also given good boots to wear.

Having fun

Victorian children didn't have playstations or televisions to watch. They entertained themselves playing with their toys and other children in games like hopscotch and tag. Children had lots of freedom and had fun playing with their friends away from adults.

Toys

Victorian children had fewer toys than children today. Poor families made their own toys such as peg dolls or bought cheap toys such as spinning tops or marbles. Wealthy children were given expensive toys like rocking horses, dolls houses, tin soldiers and clockwork trains.

◀ Victorian dolls had china faces, real hair and fancy clothes and were very expensive. This doll would have been owned by a wealthy Victorian child.

VICTORIAN LEGACY

Victorian stories

Reading was popular with Victorian families. Children enjoyed reading books such as *Alice in Wonderland*, *The Jungle Book*, *Treasure Island*, *Black beauty* and *The Water Babies*. We still read these books written by Victorian authors today. Some of these stories tell us about what life was like in Victorian times.

All the fun of the fair

The travelling fairs and circuses that moved from town to town were popular with children. They had fun visiting the stalls and side shows and taking a turn on rides, such as the gallopers and gondolas. When circuses arrived in a town they paraded through the streets showing off their elephants, caged lions and acrobats. Children earned free tickets to see the show by handing out adverts for the circus to people in the street.

▶ Fairground rides were powered by steam.

▲ Wealthy children enjoyed watching pantomimes and plays.

Pantomime time

Going to the theatre was popular in Victorian times. Every year wealthy children enjoyed going to the Christmas pantomime to see shows about *Cinderella*, *Dick Whittington* or *Robin Hood*. At home, children put on their own show in toy theatres.

On holiday

In early Victorian times, working children worked every day of the year except for Sundays, Christmas Day and Good Friday. New laws gave them Saturday afternoons off and then four Bank Holidays a year - Boxing Day, one day at Easter, Whit Monday and the first Monday in August.

Sunday school trips

For some children, their only trip out each year was with their Sunday school. Children wore their best clothes for the day, and travelled by train or in horse draw wagons loaned by local businesses. They went to the countryside or the seaside where they played games and had a picnic tea.

▼ These children are enjoying their Sunday school outing.

▼ On May Day children wove the ribbons into patterns as they danced around a pole.

May Day

On 1st May, May Day celebrations were held in the countryside. Victorian country children danced around a may pole holding ribbons. One lucky girl was chosen to be the May Queen. She was given a garland of flowers to wear in her hair and took part in a parade through the streets.

Beside the sea

Trips to the seaside became popular as travelling to the coast became quicker and cheaper on the new railways. Families went on day trips, or if they could afford to, stayed in seaside boarding houses for a week or two. Victorian children enjoyed making sand castles, paddling, watching Punch and Judy shows and having donkey rides - just like many children do today.

▼ Victorian children kept most of their clothes on at the seaside.

SIFTING THE EVIDENCE

Health and pleasure

Posters advertising seaside towns encouraged Victorians to spend their holidays there. Posters advertised places such as Blackpool as a good place for health and pleasure. It listed the attractions holiday makers can enjoy such as the Winter gardens, promenade, aquarium and two piers.

Activities

Why not experience some of the things that Victorian children did, by trying some of these activities?

Copper plate writing

Copperplate was a very impressive style of handwriting that was quite popular in the 19th century. It was started when handwriting manuals were engraved on copper plates. The engraver, in an attempt to display his/her skill, would write with swirling, complex curves and this enhanced the beauty of the writing considerably.

Victorian children practised copper plate handwriting at school by copying out sentences from copybooks. The sentences were often short moral sayings about behaviour such as 'Time and tide wait for no man' and 'Waste not want not'.
Try your hand at writing like a Victorian by copying these sentences in your best handwriting.

Unpruned vines never bear good fruit.
Unpruned vines never bear good fruit.
Unpruned vines never bear good fruit.
Unpruned vines never bear good fruit.

Use the means and wait for the blessing
Use the means and wait for the blessing.
Use the means and wait for the blessing.
Use the means and wait for the blessing

Cook like a Victorian

Mrs Beeton wrote a recipe book for Victorian housewives. She recommended this recipe for children. Why not try making it?

Baked rice pudding (adapted)
Ingredients
- 50 g of pudding rice
- 2 tablespoons of sugar
- 500 ml milk
- 15 g butter
- half a teaspoon of ground
- nutmeg

Wash the rice in a sieve with cold running water.

Put the rice in a pie dish. Add the sugar and milk and stir well.

Cut the butter into small pieces and add to the rice mixture. Sprinkle the nutmeg on top.

Bake at 150°C for 1 1/2 - 2 hours until the rice is soft.

Bowling a hoop

Victorian children played with metal hoops in the streets. They pushed the hoop along by repeatedly hitting it with a stick to keep it rolling, as they ran alongside. Try this game with a modern plastic hoop and a short piece of stick such as bamboo.

Make a peg doll

Poor Victorian children played with simple homemade peg dolls. Use a traditional wooden dolly clothes peg, scraps of wool and material to make your own peg doll. Draw or paint a face on one side of the round end of the peg. Glue pieces of wool on to the other side of the peg top to make the doll's hair. Wrap a square of material around the rest of the peg to make the clothes.

Blind man's wand

Parlour games were popular with Victorian children. The game of Blind man's wand is easy and fun to play for four or more children. All you need is a blindfold and a stick.

Choose one person to be the blind man and put a blindfold on them. The blind man then holds out a stick and another child holds the opposite end. The blind man asks the person holding the other end of the stick, three questions, with the aim of finding out who they are. The person answering the questions should disguise their voice to stop the blind man guessing correctly. If the blind man guesses correctly then the other person becomes the blind man.

Timeline

1837 Victoria becomes queen.

1840 Chimney Sweep Act tries to stop children being sent up chimneys - it fails.

1842 Mines Act stops girls and boys under the age of ten working underground in coal mines.

1844 Factory Act limits children under thirteen to working $6^{1/2}$ hours a day. Dangerous machinery has to be fenced in.

1847 Factory Act reduces the working week for children under eighteen to no more than 58 hours.

1860 Mines Act raises starting age to twelve for children working underground.

1865 *Alice in Wonderland* published.

1867 Factory Act - all workers on a 10-hour day.

1870 Education Act sets up board schools for five-to-ten year olds - there is a small fee.

1870 Dr Barnardo opens first home for homeless boys.

1871 First Bank holidays.

1873 Agricultural Act stops children under eight working on farms.

1875 Lord Shaftesbury's Chimney Sweep Act stops children working as chimney sweeps - it succeeds.

1878 Factory and Workshops Act stops employment of children under ten years old.

1883 *Treasure Island* published.

1884 NSPCC founded to stop children being cruelly treated.

1891 New law makes free schooling compulsory for all children between the age of five and thirteen.

1901 Queen Victoria dies, her son becomes King Edward VII.

Glossary and further information

census information collected about all the people living in Britain. It is taken every ten years.

copybook a book with printed examples of good handwriting that children had to copy out to practice their writing.

domestic skills skills such as washing, ironing, cleaning and cooking.

drill a physical education (PE) lesson, where children had to jump, bend, stretch as the teacher shouted out instructions.

governess a woman paid to teach wealthy children at home.

hops plants used to flavour beer.

industrial nation a country that has lots of factories for making things.

legacy something handed down from the past and still used today.

logbook school diary used by the headteacher.

NSPCC the shortened name of the charity National Society for the Prevention of Cruelty to Children.

peg doll a simple doll made from a wooden clothes peg and scraps of fabric.

privy an outside toilet, often in a shed with a hole or bucket underneath a wooden seat.

reciting when a person says the same thing over and over again.

statesmen men who work in the government and rule the country.

Sunday school Church school on Sunday morning where children learned stories from the Bible.

transported taken by ship to another country as punishment for a crime.

Whit Monday The day after Whit Sunday, a religious holiday seven weeks after Easter.

Further information

There are many museums and websites you can visit to find out more about Victorian children. Local museums often run events about life in Victorian times.

www.nationaltrust.org.uk
The National Trust has a Museum of Childhood at Sudbury Hall, Derbyshire, and a workhouse at Southwell in Nottinghamshire.

www.learningcurve.gov.uk
Look at records from the National Archives to find out about Victorian children in trouble.

www.raggedschoolmuseum.org.uk
The Ragged Schools Museum in London has a Victorian classroom.

www.vam.ac.uk/moc/index.html
The V&A Museum of Childhood in London has displays of Victorian children's toys, games and clothes.

Index